My Joys & Sorrows

AS A MOTHER OF A SPECIAL CHILD

My Joys & Sorrows

AS A MOTHER OF A SPECIAL CHILD

Dr. Krishna Saksena

Ocean Books
Pvt. Ltd.

Published by
Ocean Books (P) Ltd.
4/19 Asaf Ali Road,
New Delhi-110 002 (INDIA)
e-mail: info@oceanbooks.in

ISBN 978-81-8430-631-6
MY JOYS & SORROWS
by Dr. Krishna Saksena

Edition
First, 2021

Price
₹ 300.00 (Rupees Three Hundred only)

Printed at
Nakshatra Art, New Delhi

This book is dedicated to Prabha Jauhari, my bhabhi, friend and confidant, who was taken away by the Lord this year. I will miss her gentle smile and her selfless love.

PREFACE

I was surprised to find myself crying as I read the book. Surprised because I do not easily cry and after all this is just a book. But it is much more than just a book. It is a rare glimpse into the depth of love and pain of a mother for her handicapped son. The scriptures say that to look for a near-perfect relationship in this world, one must examine the relationship of a mother with her child. Near-perfect because there is still a tinge of expectation. The mother expects the child to take care of her in her old age. But here we have a mother who is completely aware that there was no possibility of her son ever taking care of her. On the contrary, she understands that this is a burden for her to bear for the rest of her life. Yet it does nothing to diminish her love and care for the son. On the contrary it only increases her desire to protect him, support him and ensure his comfort. Even to the extent that she chooses to neglect her other children.

Yet there is no resentment. Only regret that she could have done more and could have done better. All the pains that the son suffered were experienced many times over by the mother. We see her purposefully diminishing her relationships with her other children just to nurture the one with her handicapped son. That is the glory of this relationship. It is pure and simple love, uncontaminated by any expectation or ulterior motive.

I want to thank Dr. Krishna Saksena for giving us a glimpse into this deep and intimate aspect of her life, for allowing to us to witness love in its purest form and for showing us the power of faith. The book has been written in an easy, conversational style and draws you in as if you are actually fortunate to be sitting right next to her and hearing from her.

There are no attempts made by the author to glorify herself, there is no efforts to get recognition for her sacrifices and absolutely no desire to elicit any pity. It is a reflection of the beautiful and selfless relationship she has with her son.

This is a book that needs to read over and over because with every read one realizes a more nuanced aspect of this wonderful relationship of unconditional love in its most pristine form.

— **Indu Adawal**

My Joys & Sorrows

Life is a battle which comes with challenges every day. One has to fight and face it. What is needed is the courage to fight them and not to shy

away. Instead of saying, "I have failed" say, "I have not succeeded so far". What you need to do is to remember the Mother Divine and this will give strength to your mind and you will have fresh energy (Swami Vivekanand).

I need to be confident of who I am. Being deeply loved gives strength, while loving someone gives courage (Lao Tzu). The confidence one builds from

> The confidence one builds from achieving difficult things and accomplishing goals is the most difficult and the most beautiful things of all.

achieving difficult things and accomplishing goals is the most difficult and the most beautiful things of all. Numerous relations exist, but the one that of mother and her son is the best. If you ask me the reason it will be difficult to tell. Geeta of *Uddhav* tells us so.

I was married to a Class One Officer. I had four children—three sons and one daughter. The eldest is Shanker, next is Tanya, a daughter, next to her is my son, Bali and the youngest son is *Shiv*. I was working as a lecturer in one of the colleges of Delhi University. From a travelling job, my husband got a post as a Director on the civil side. To change the station after every few months was not good. It was harmful and quite difficult as far the studies of our children and our jobs were concerned. It was a time when we laughed shared jokes and enjoyed happy banter. I would host parties and my house was a place where anyone was free to come in and enjoy our company.

But this good time did not last long. After three years measles broke in the shape of an epidemic. It affected children badly. Many died and Shiv our youngest, fell its prey. It took a very ugly form. He lost the balance of his head and the most beautiful child took a very ugly form. He would hit anyone with his head that would come before him, so hard that it would hurt the person badly. People stopped coming to my place. They laughed at us. In the life you have challenges.

In the life you have challenges. You can face them.

You can face them. It was so funny when Shiv would hit anyone with his head that came before him. It looked so odd. He did not understand what was wrong being so small just one year old. They laughed at us. They hated us and kept a distance from us. The little child could not tell his problem while all hated him and even went to the extent to beat him.

Just next to my house there was a set of three small rooms. In one was a beautiful marble statue of Mother Divine. The other two were used as a stop gap by saints, pandits and learned men.

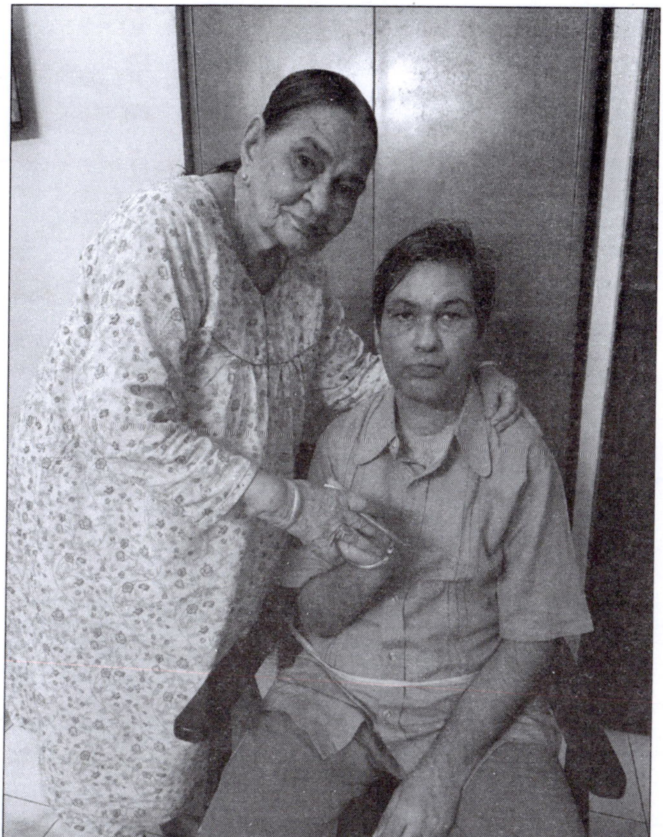

They would stay for a day or two and proceed on to their journey. One day, a saint saw me, my tears and my child folding my hands before my Divine Ma. After arti, the saint came to me and spoke softly and lovingly 'Life is a battle which comes with challenges. You can express your pain but what about the little one who is being punished by all for his pain". I was quiet but he continued, 'You are a mother in motherhood, a state higher than heavens.

They would stay for a day or two and proceed on to their journey.

You know my dear we worship persons like you". I was quiet but he continued for I could not speak before a great man. He said, "Remember who you are? Take the name of your Divine Ma, say AUM as you get up in the morning and with a smile of gratitude, start the day. I am sure you will win. You think I do

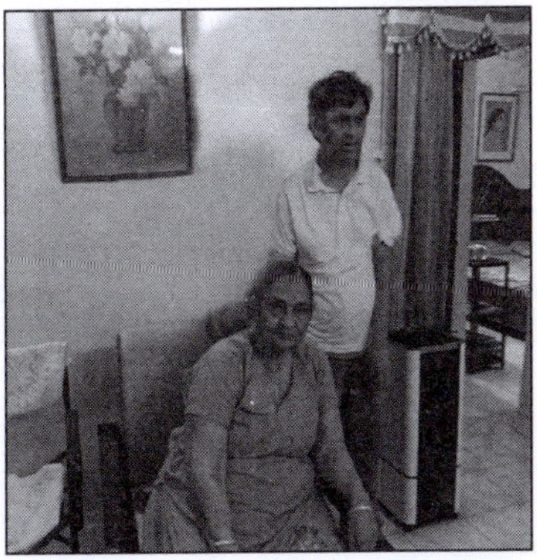

not know your problem. My dear I am well aware of it. It should not disturb you. He too loves you which you do not take in account. So both of you he repeated, so both of you are standing in the same line. Remember Ma and be happy with your lot". Saying this, he got up and went inside.

Remember Ma and be happy with your lot". Saying this, he got up and went inside.

Every one close to me had pity over my condition and that hurt me even more. Sugges- tions came from all sides

I should admit him in a hospital and be free.

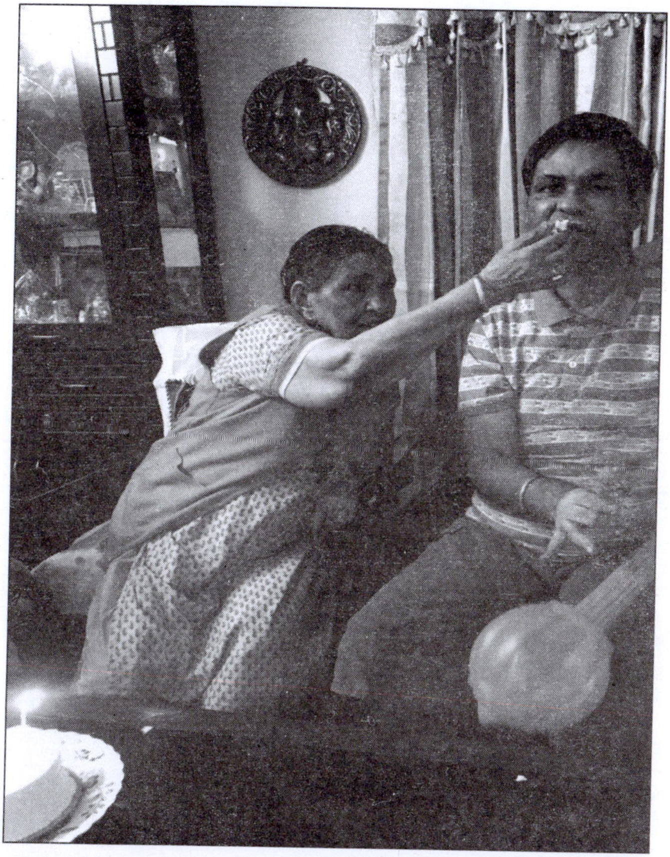

that I should admit him in a hospital and be free. I refused to do so and did not let my child go away from me. One allopathic doctor at *Golmarket* taking me in confidence told me that he had a magical injection which if given will make him to go off to sleep forever. I took my child and ran out. My husband had faith in astrology and he spent lot of money giving to those who fooled him telling him that he would make his child all right. Nobody had any feeling for him. All wanted a life of ease and com-

> All wanted a life of ease and comfort.

fort. One moment, I felt as others, to put him away and live a life of ease but the next moment I would hold him to my heart and tears would fill my eyes and I did not know what I wanted. A great pandit observed me and came near me and spoke softly, "I have been observing you, often seeing you, I may tell you that so long as we believe in our heart of hearts that our capacity is limited and we grow anxious and unhappy we are lacking in faith. One who truly trusts in God has no right to be anxious about anything". (*Param-hans*)

It was the mental disease of Shiv that led him to run as long as he was awake, he would run out as soon as the gate was found open, hit the person with his head if he saw one. Shiv always accompanied me when I went to the temple in the morning to bend down as I started the day to say AUM and in the evening for arti. Shiv would say in his own style. We were particular about keeping outer door closed for if found open, Shiv would run out. When his voice was not heard all would run out to bring him back. Once not hearing his voice, his brothers ran out but they could not sec him. Then his sister ran out and saw him smiling and holding fast a cow's tail and looking around to make sure that no body was coming to catch him. His brother then caught him and took him inside.

When his voice was not heard all would run out to bring him back. When his voice was not heard all would run out to bring him back.

Once during the hot summer, all of us were sleeping outside on the verandah. In the quiet of the dark night, he got up and started walking. There was a staircase. He continued his walk. He tumbled down, and rolling he touched the ground. An officer brought him to us. We then began to sleep indoors in that hot season. Once I had gone to the college, it was raining hard when Shiv in his pram stood up.

> In the quiet of the dark night, he got up and started walking.

The ayah was busy talking to her friend. Shiv got up and climbed on the railing and jumped from the first floor to the ground. He ought to have died but he stood up and started walking. The ayah scared, ran away. I was naturally summoned and I took him to the hospital where he was seen and examined and found there was not a scratch and he was unharmed.

He ought to have died but he stood up and started walking. The ayah scared, ran away.

To fight courageously means to face the life which is our lot. We confront problems that are difficult. If the love within your mind is lost and you see other beings as enemies then no matter how much knowledge or education or material comfort you have, only suffering and confusion will ensue. (Dalai Lama). Try your best and you will find that this is the shortest way to benevolence. You should love your neighbor as yourself. You should not behave in such a manner which is disagreeable to one self. This is the essence of morality.

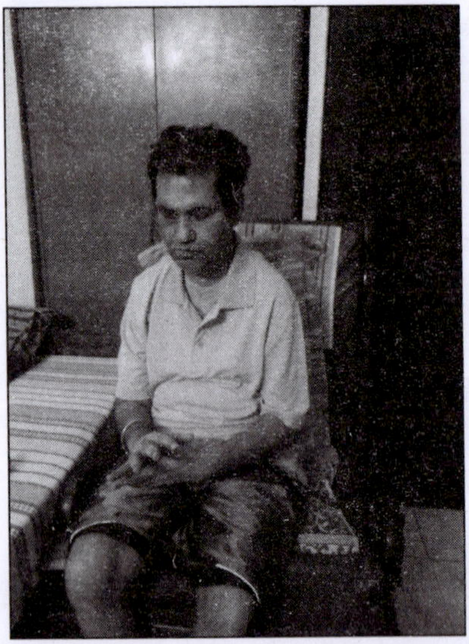

You should not behave in such a manner which hurts anyone. This is the most important thing. All other activities are due to selfish desires. All men should go about treating creatures as he himself would like to be treated. This should be our aim. But we are all very selfish ones looking only to our conveniences.

Shiv would repeat with me in his own funny way Om and Jai Mata. All would laugh at him. But for me it is a great day July 19,1964, Shiv's birthday. It is a special day that has changed the very direction of my life. I have learnt great lessons

> It is a special day that has changed the very direction of my life.

that he gave, I started loving him more than any other of my children. My Mother Divine held my hand and said, "Come on with me". Through Shiv, She showed the world and its people and taught me to live, love and laugh.

Shiv would run after me wherever I went. Speaking in his own funny way, jumping, dancing he would make himself a laughing stock. With him they would start hating me. They would make fun of me and jeered at me. Silently I was bearing all this. I was bearing all this but sitting alone with Shiv tears would flow, little Shiv would run to wipe my tears with his shirt. This would make me to smile. But all friends jeered at me. The group was broken. Now they hesitated to even look at me. The joy of the group vanished and we became a laughing stock.

Those I termed as my best friend refused to talk to me fearing that she may catch the disease that

Those I termed as my best friend refused to talk to me fearing that she may catch the disease that Shiv had.

❖ Dr. Krishna Saksena ❖

Shiv had. Friends are tested in such times and I could well see the truth of the statement. I could well see Divine Ma had put well all the miseries of the world in my bag. I had to carry it as there was no other way out. All went for enjoyment and entertainment but I had to be left behind to look after Shiv. My other children complained that I did not love them, the only one that I loved was Shiv. I tried to convince them that "I love all of you but I care more for Shiv because he does not understand anything. He cannot take care of himself". But sitting alone I would always weep thinking of what sins I have committed that I have been treated this way by the Divine. My husband tried to console me by saying, if I have been given one like Shiv, She has given three sweet intelligent children. "I would say it is easy to say than go through it. No argument is good enough".

A day when all of us were going out with Shiv, he was running fast and crossed the road. A tonga

A day when all of us were going out with Shiv, he was running fast and crossed the road.

coming at a very fast speed could not stop to let Shiv cross. It passed over him. All on the road were sure that Shiv would be dead but to everyone's surprise Shiv stood and started running. All on the street— the cobbler, fruit seller, the one selling flowers remember Shiv whenever they see me.

I thanked my mother *Ambe*. "Gratitude arises whenever you start feeling God's presence around you; then only gratitude is felt then your whole energy becomes thanks giving it becomes a prayer". Shiv and myself went to the temple and fell on the feet of Ma. One moment I felt so angry with Shiv that I felt like slapping him and another moment felt like holding him tight to my heart. Tears came in my eyes and started flowing down. A saint that was watching me said "I have been often seeing you and observing you. I may tell you so long as we believe in our heart of hearts that our capacity is limited and we grow anxious and unhappy we are lacking in faith. One who truly trust in God has no right to be anxious about anything". (*Paramhans yoganand*)

Shiv created new problems every time. In the name of curing him so many cheated me. Magicians, *vaids*, pandits and hakims assured me that they had put right even more serious patients than Shiv in no time and charged heavy amounts for treating Shiv with no gains.

Life was moving with its ups and downs when came an important event, the marriage of my daughter. As usual was the practice, Shiv was put in a room and locked from outside. I forgot to lock the door of the bathroom inside. Shiv opened the door and slipped as the ground was all wet. His head stuck the pipe and started bleeding profusely and he cried loudly. I opened the door and saw what had happened. The baraat was on the gate how I could have gone away to the hospital. By chance amongst our guests was a nurse who bandaged him and saved the situation. But this incident totally turned my mood off and the event passed without any enjoyment.

His head stuck the pipe and started bleeding profusely and he cried loudly.

Special

Shiv was fond of only two persons—his mummy and his daddy. All the time that his father was at home, his favorite Shiv would be with him riding on his back or taking food with him. With me he would lie down next to me and hold me tight to go off to sleep. All was so enjoyable. He hated his ayah because behind our back she would beat him severely. Life moved with its ups and downs and it was my faith in my Mother Divine that made me happy.

With Shiv, every day something would happen that would take away the very spirit of my existence. One day Shiv was playing in the small garden that was in front of my house. He not only looked normal but very pretty and handsome. The ayah had gone inside to drink water. A child lifter saw him and finding the gate unlocked came inside

One day Shiv was playing in the small garden that was in front of my house.

❖ Dr. Krishna Saksena ❖

and carried him away. The ayah came inside and gave us the news. I told her to get out. You can come if my Shiv comes else you can go back to the place from where you have come. I was so hurt. The Police were alerted. The police commissioner at that time was a relation of mine to whom I made the request to find Shiv with tears flowing down. My husband and myself started looking at places where we thought Shiv could be. I came to the temple and with folded hands begged MA to give back our Shiv. In sheer desperation I

❖ Dr. Krishna Saksena ❖

started crying. Shortly, several calls from different police stations began to come and ascertain, for a child of my description was found and I could come and see if it is mine. I went to five police stations at their call, but it was never my Shiv. I gave up the idea to get my child back. My other children did not get anything to eat. So Bali said "Mummy let us forget him and at least have some tea". I scolded him. Shiv has not been found and you are thinking of

I went to five police stations at their call, but it was never my Shiv.

❖ DR. KRISHNA SAKSENA ❖

tea. Poor thing after been scolded he was quiet. A call came at about eight o'clock asking us to come and see a child that had been brought just then. I was very tired and so I asked the havildar to call him by the name of Shiv and if he responds we will come. He replied that the child is too disturbed that he is not in a mood to respond. I told my husband that let us go and see. We told the havildar to keep that man who brought him sitting till we come. We went and saw Shiv sitting disturbed and silent. I quickly picked him up and asked for the man who brought him up. He looked at

❖ Dr. Krishna Saksena ❖

the chair next to him but the sadhu had disappeared. Five minutes back he was there. He sent men to look for him for he could not be beyond the gate but to the surprise of all he could not be seen for miles. I came back with Shiv first thanking my great Ma then all others who helped me in my search of my child. His ayah came running on seeing Shiv. You can understand a mother's delight. Shiv could not answer any question because he could not understand why he was taken away and put to so much of torture.

Next day when I went to the temple, I sat with a face that has been crushed and tortured. The saint asked "any trouble". I told him all that had happened. He smiled and said "life has been compared to a battle and rightly so as each day comes up with a new set of challenges which we must meet. One cannot shy away from problems if he has to survive. You have to meet the challenges with courage". He then softly put his hand on my head and went inside. I felt relieved to a great extent.

Shiv would go out on his pram every day driven by his servant. One day I accompanied Shiv. We had gone to some distance when a young man stopped me and asked "Is this your child". I said "yes". "Has he got some brain problem?" "Yes" I replied. "You come with me and I will show you my shop and the bottle is only for Rs 20000/per bottle. You have to use it for a week after which if you need a

We had gone to some distance when a young man stopped me and asked "Is this your child".

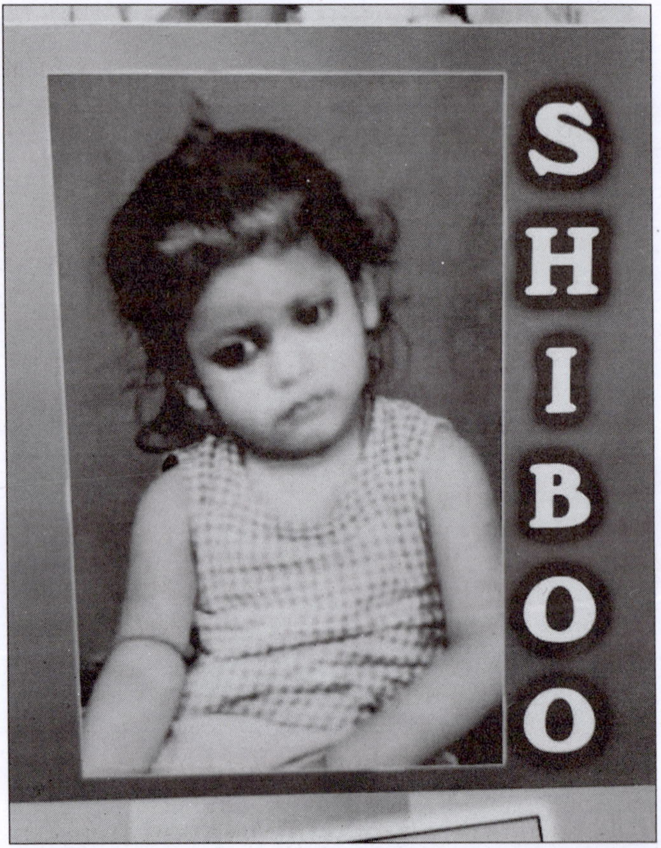
SHIBOO

little more you can come here and get it. But I am sure, looking at his condition, you will not need more. You can see those that are coming need only a little more after the first bottle. I thought if I asked my husband he will say that they are cheats, keep away. So I quietly came home took out Rs.20,000 and bought the bottle and came home. I kept on applying for six days without an inch of improvement so on the seventh day I went to his shop. A number of men were sitting who had been fooled like me. The shop had disappeared and the man was nowhere to be found. I could be fooled to any extent if Shiv was in question. We got the news that the treatment by brain surgery had finally come to India. A lady doctor dealing with brain problems in G.B. Pant hospital told us that we can take Shiv to Madras for the operation. My husband even gave extra money to the doctor who was going to operate so that he may perform the operation with care to be success and put Shiv right. We were happy that if we could not take him to a foreign country for treatment, at least we could take him to Madras. At this time my husband was holding the post of Director of training. So many young boys were under him. In too much of hurry and enthusiasm I forgot to bow before my Divine Ma before departure. The young boys came to greet their teacher and when they saw Shiv, they requested my husband to take Shiv and get him blessed by *Shankracharya.* He had no objection. So they took Shiv and came to *maharaj ji*. I also went with them. Maharaj ji was sitting on the ground only wearing a dhoti. A boy spoke in a very sweet submissive tone, "Baba this child has come for your blessings for he is being operated tomorrow". Baba put his hand in the basket and was about to take the apple to give as *ashirwad* when his hand was stuck. He then turned and had a close look at Shiv he

I also went with them. Maharaj ji was sitting on the ground only wearing a dhoti.

dropped the apple and sat down quietly without doing anything, without giving the apple, it meant without giving him his blessing making it evident that Shiv's operation will be an utter fail ure. The boys then came back with Shiv. The next day the operation was performed and his body became so stiff that it could hardly be straightened. All the junior doctors started massaging his body but it

The boys then came back with Shiv.

made no difference what so ever. The question arose of how he could be taken home in that awful condition. All of us were sitting in the veranda talking about what was to be done when all of a sudden, a figure came out and started running. We wondered who it could be, on a closer look We found it was none but our little Shiv. We quickly bought the tickets and came back to Delhi. It was at this time that I remembered my own

The question arose of how he could be taken home in that awful condition.

Mother Divine whose blessings I forgot to take. But now it was too late.

Now was the time that my husband retired and he had to leave the accommodation. I had seen in the village of *Bawana* at a reasonable rate, land there which I bought and built a beautiful bungalow where Shiv would roam about happily. Even if he fell down, he would get up and start roaming again. No slaps, no dragging about he was so happy. But it meant a

Even if he fell down, he would get up and start roaming again.

lot of trouble and a long distance for my college. But the happiness of Shiv was my happiness. Shankar who was interested in doing business started one. It flourished for sometime. My husband started disliking the place because poor people were living all around so he had no good company around. I was happy so was Shiv. But when Holi came all of us sang and danced and had lovely things to eat. This time my *aya's* husband had come. He was a famous confectioner. So, a lot of sweets

> I was happy so was Shiv.

were made. This happy moment was a great moment for all of us. We got lovely things to eat. My husband ate a lot, everything that was in a tin. I lost my temper when I came back from a staff council meeting and saw the tin empty. Next day he started vomiting so badly that two rooms were badly soiled. I called the doctor. By chance Ajay my, son -in- law and my daughter also came up. The doctor examined the patient and told Ajay either to stay back or carry the patient with him. He decided to take my husband away to his place.

On the way to the hospital, he got him examined and was found that he had a severe heart attack. He took him to the hospital, got him admitted in his hospital under the care of a good heart specialist. He requested the crowd of friends and relation should not disturb him. Stunts were inserted but charred lungs did not give much support because he was a heavy smoker.

He requested the crowd of friends and relation should not disturb him.

Renu stayed with him for the whole day and he very much liked her company. Shankar and myself looked after Shiv and also food. He kept on asking for Bali. He asked about him so many times that I finally disgusted had to tell him that he has left for foreign country and from there he cannot come at a short notice. "But have you given the notice?" I nodded my head. He then asked for Shiv. I said "HE will jump on you and move on to other bed". He smiled remembering him. He said I feel so hurt that I have to leave you alone in the middle of a journey that has nothing but obstacles". It did not take much time and he passed away. Despite the best efforts of the doctors, he could not live. The hospital was so unlucky. Tears rolled down my cheeks.

Despite the best efforts of the doctors, he could not live.

The dead body was handed to me. I hired a truck that carried the dead body and put in the body of my husband. Shanker was scared to sit alone with the dead so I also sat with Shanker.

Reaching home, we called in a pandit, the necessary formalities were completed, the body was taken in the same truck. None of the relations came but the people of the entire village sat. The body was immersed in *GarhGanga*. We moved away from *Bawana*. A rented accommodation was taken. I took a woman from *Bawana* to look after Shiv. The people who were to bring the luggage to the new place were told that in no case anything from the puja room needs to be brought, because after the death of my husband I had gone through a severe attack of depression. I lost faith in my Mother Divine as I sat through the whole night and would get not a wink of sleep. I was sure that henceforth in my house She will find no place. Within me there was a volcanic eruption and I could not control myself. I cried and cried at any time to

Within me there was a volcanic eruption and I could not control myself.

put off my grief. I thought of my Divine Ma and asked her if this was the result of loving Her. I raised the voice against the injustice done to me. Ma I cannot take it as a part of my destiny. I wonder why a sweet mother can be so unkind. I was in my small temple gone to register my grief when by chance I met my old saint. I got up and touched his feet. He blessed me. I told him my story wiping tears from my eyes. The saint sat down by my side and putting his hand on my back said, "Lift yourself up with the help of yourself. You can be your best guide, philosopher and friend and you can be your worst enemy. Doing puja will help you greatly". For me this hospital remains very unlucky. Tears rolled down my cheeks, and I asked Ma "IS this the result of all my prayers and love for you? Should not people raise their voice against the injustice that is done to me? Or do I have to take quietly

Doing puja will help you greatly". For me this hospital remains very unlucky.

as a part of my destiny? Why is it that Ma is so quiet and unkind some times? I cried loudly for I could not control myself. The saint tried to console, "My dear, do not be discouraged by a failure for failure is the way to success.

> He patted her back and got up to go inside.

He patted her back and got up to go inside. He turned back and asked, "Where is my little one?" "We have taken a rented house which is far away". He smiled and went inside.

Have I done puja for no good? My tears would not stop despite my best efforts. Shanker, my eldest son resigned from his job to be with me. In all facets of my life public or private he was seen holding my hands. The younger one also helped me whenever his turn came. The youngest one Shiv was one that changed the very course of my life. Bali approved of a girl with whom he was going to get married.

The younger one also helped me whenever his turn came.

With a grand band the marriage party started. The bridegroom sat in the car and next to him was his elder brother. The car moved slowly accompanied by the band. A voice rose where is the mother. A telephone call came "Come fast everyone is asking for you". I put on a saree, and requested the landlord to ask her servant to look after Shiv. I reached the place where all were happy to see me. Formalities were performed. Soon I

A telephone call came "Come fast everyone is asking for you".

came back and to my surprise Shiv had just gone down the stairs and the person who was requested to look after him was fast asleep on the sofa.

My mind had only two things anger and hatred. Why was it that my husband was taken away? What wrong had I done to get this punishment? First as a mother I had one son like Shiv that took away from me the pleasures of young age. There was no company for me except

What wrong had I done to get this punishment?

loneliness and sorrow. In loneliness I could not control myself. In the share of one there was so much of pain. To release this pain I wanted to cry loudly. Sometimes when everyone was beating Shiv I would feel very sorry and cry. I felt if he did some wrong, he was lacking in understanding but why those very intelligent should react so badly as to hit him so hard. From all sides there was with me nothing but pain. I wanted to leave my job, take Shiv and run away to some remote place. Even in the college every one kept on asking me, "What has gone wrong with you?" Life looked so dull and painful, I felt like committing suicide, but the face of Shiv would not allow me to do so. Things looked dismal, I wanted to cry loudly to ease the pain of heart. I sought my soul, but my soul I could not see. I sought my husband but he seemed to be running away. My heart broke and I looked on all sides to find hope somewhere but I was disappointed.

Things looked dismal, I wanted to cry loudly to ease the pain of heart.

Guest of hono
Smt Smriti Zubi
extiles and & Minister of Wom
2019

ok Launch
ers of Time

In such a disturbed mood I saw lot of dust under the bed of Shiv so I thought I might clean it so I went to get the broom. A number of things were piled up on a shelf. When I took out one, something red was seen under it. I became curious to see what it was. To my surprise I saw the photograph of my Mother Divine. "Oh, Ma what have I done?" "You left me but how can I leave my devotee. Stand up, hold your head high and walk with a determination to defeat your destiny". Her words gave me lot of encouragement. I came to a

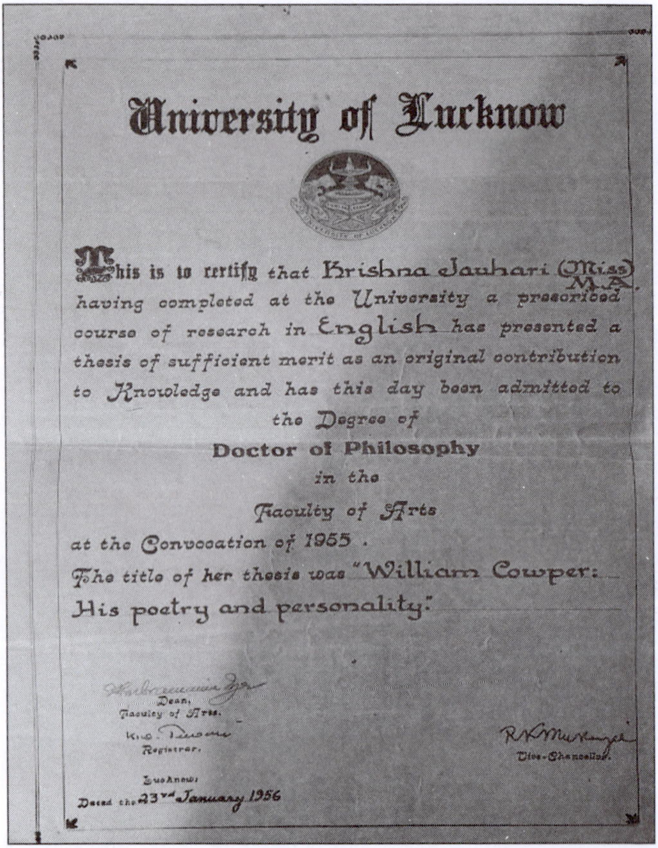

University of Lucknow

This is to certify that Krishna Jauhari (Miss) M.A.
having completed at the University a prescribed course of research in English has presented a thesis of sufficient merit as an original contribution to Knowledge and has this day been admitted to
the Degree of
Doctor of Philosophy
in the
Faculty of Arts
at the Convocation of 1955.
The title of her thesis was "William Cowper: His poetry and personality."

Dean,
Faculty of Arts.

Registrar.

Vice-Chancellor.

Lucknow:
Dated the 23rd January 1956

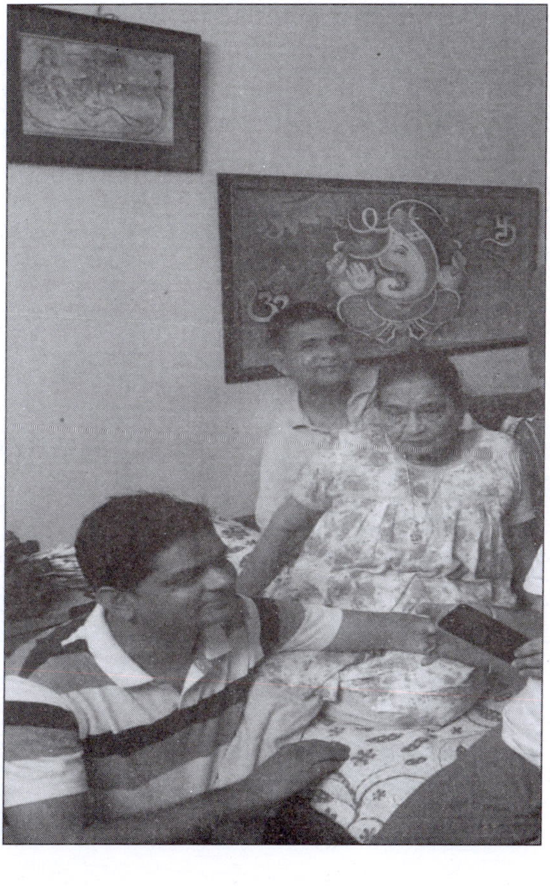

कुमारी कृष्णा जोहरी एम० ए०
लखनऊ विश्वविद्यालय की प्रथम

MISS KRISHNA JAUHARI AWARDED PH. D. DEGREE

Miss Krishna Jauhari, M.A., has

Miss Krishna Jauhari, who has been awarded the Ph.D. in English by Lucknow

कुमारी कृष्णा जोहरी

आप लखनऊ विश्वविद्यालय की
प्रथम छात्रा हैं जिनको उत्तर प्रदेश

small room that was empty and spread a piece of satin cloth and put the photograph there. I also lit an oil lamp and *agarbatti* next to Her. I folded my hands and begged of her to give me strength, peace and happiness. I followed my Mother's orders and I was another person strong, smiling, and moving fast in life.

He suffered serious illness twice, a third being a prey to the deadly disease, Covid, when even his doctor gave up all hopes. His brothers stood as

rock behind him. His doctor, famous Dr. Manoj Kumar Goel, Director Fortis Memorial Research Institute, also took great interest in treating him and got him well. His mother prayed for him. Our efforts rose high and he came out every time better than before. Today he sits smiling, folding his hands to greet you.

❖❖❖